Rúben Alexandre Pinto Rocha is a writer born in 1991 in Lisbon, son of Ivone Luís Pinto and Manuel do Carmo Monteiro Rocha. He studied Hospitality and Tourism, and has been distinguished by the publication of several books: *Burning Flame* (Editions Vieira da Silva) and *The Hand of God* (Corpus Publishing company).

I dedicate this book to my mother, Ivone Pinto, João Landim, Carolina Pinto, Viteche Meggi and Carla Rebelo, because without you it would not be possible to elaborate it.

Dark Angel

DREAMS

AUSTIN MACAULEY PUBLISHERS™
LONDON • CAMBRIDGE • NEW YORK • SHARJAH

Copyright © Dark Angel 2024

The right of Dark Angel to be identified as author of this work has been asserted by the author in accordance with sections 77 and 78 of the Copyright, Designs and Patents Act 1988.

All rights reserved. No part of this publication may be reproduced, stored in a retrieval system, or transmitted in any form or by any means, electronic, mechanical, photocopying, recording, or otherwise, without the prior permission of the publishers.

Any person who commits any unauthorized act in relation to this publication may be liable to criminal prosecution and civil claims for damages.

A CIP catalogue record for this title is available from the British Library.

ISBN 9781528922401 (Paperback)
ISBN 9781528922418 (Hardback)
ISBN 9781528963770 (ePub e-book)

www.austinmacauley.com

First Published 2024
Austin Macauley Publishers Ltd®
1 Canada Square
Canary Wharf
London
E14 5AA

Table of Contents

Introduction	9
Dreams	10
Weaknesses	13
The Legacy	15
Die and Live	18
Incomprehension	20
The Inner Change	23
The Seal of Love	26
The Spirit of a Winner	29
A Word to Say	33
The Forgiveness	36
The Impossible Dream	39
Love Tears	41
Flames and Certainties	44
Fight for Love	47
The Use of Reason	49

The Life of Peace	**51**
Mistrust	**53**
The Life of a Champion	**56**
The Power of True Dream	**58**
The Greatness of Love	**60**
The Truth of a Dream	**63**
The Usefulness of Life	**66**
Love	**68**
The Difficult Times	**70**
The Power of Imagination	**72**
The Fellow Love	**76**
The Power of True Love	**78**
The Certainty of the Realization of Dreams	**80**
The Right Woman: God's Best Gift	**82**
The Power of the True Dream	**84**

Introduction

No one lives without dreams, they are the power that gives strength to the weak, they reinvigorate the depressed, they raise the fallen, they are the hope of those who fight without hope or when there is no confidence left to believe, to fight and even to survive. This work shows what poetry means to me: one of my great dreams!

The air I breathe, the universe in which I live, the breath of life that is in me, passed through poems and convictions that accompany me daily. Just as a child is generated, I have carefully designed this book in order to offer the best of myself. Dreams resist the no, and mine is to be the greatest poet of all time, growing humbly, blood, sweat and tears, but with the certainty that my work will be recognized throughout the planet through my *Dreams!*

Dreams

Every year the dream persecutes me, as the air is indispensable to live,
Ambition seizes my reason for being able to grow and take possession
From what is mine by right, without testament or royal blood,
But with God I know that I can be more than a mere mortal.

The tears flow out of the mind and slowly run through the heart,
Expressing the pain of seeing that a winner is wronged and lives to be treated
Like a thief, but no comment or prayer relieves the pain,
I put love aside and prepare to be a winner.

Many try to live at the expense of the work done by others,
But they do not withstand the pressures; they give a thousand laughter,
But then they make several tumbles, their end being a shapeless life,
That ends in the earth, inside the coffins.

Being black or white, poor or rich, beautiful or ugly,
All are born to win, but not all enjoy the best of this land, I learned that to survive, one must live in war,
To have a quality life it is necessary to do what is not asked of me,
But what is demanded by the conscience, I place upon my shoulders
The burden of responsibility of my life and I assume my failure or success.

Although it fights against armies, kings or authorities, Attitudes confirm that I was born to win
And dethrone of power who thinks himself invincible,
With injustice, people live and enjoy riches
Or enjoy seeing the misfortune of others,
But with applied certainty I actually learn to be
The greatness that gives flavour to this world,
Without accepting to overlook what I was taught.

When I have pure consciousness, I have the strength to go on,
But if she accuses me, I have no peace to sleep,
Mastering my inner self I am ready to go out and win,
If my heart is hurt, everything I do will make it an easy target to shoot down,
Because strength is born in justice and not in the strength of the arm or in the power that is possessed.

Life has two paths,
When I know that I will find thorns, I am afraid,
But I do not spare myself the effort; I know that it is through my blood that everything is acquired,
Life for life, but nothing will escape my hand,
In integrity I find mercy and in truth encounter determination,
To make any decision, certain that I am victorious wherever my foot
Dare to step on any floor!

"Dreams are individual attitudes that show the profile that exists in each person, but to be fulfilled, they demand a total surrender, whether or not they are successful, because success is always accompanied by failure. The winner must know how to win and lose, in order to have the structure to withstand all the pressures and to remain firm and unshakeable."

Weaknesses

All the tears came out from inside me; my heart bleeds
Because you do not see the solution to so much suffering,
I occupy my head and lose track of time trying to find a way out,
I know that to react is what gives meaning to life.

You can advance or retreat, fight or lose, insist or give up,
But nothing can overcome you when you face with the certainty of the value that you possess,
The air is hard to hold when I am angry, defeats consume my being,
Sometimes I become fragile, but I heal my wounds and move on,
Because I do not waste time crying for the past.

The defeats make me stronger and more mature, sure that I lost a battle,
But I did not lose the war because I live on earth and wage war,
But I lay my head on the bed, and quietly rest and attain tranquillity
That reassures my spirit and soothes my soul.

When you go through afflictions, I will be your affection,
When you are in distress, I will be your comfort,
In persecution you will have my peace, because only those who oppose the whole world will win
And choose to be true and make me your partner, so do not be afraid!

In the darkness of life I see God,
In my imperfections I see opportunity to grow
And to overcome my limitations, learning to trust and to mature,
Without ever underestimating what I learned during my journey,
Nothing is achieved with ease, what is worth requires more than necessary
And more than is required, because when we do something more, is that
We get the feeling that our duty has been fulfilled.

"What is worth conquering is the change of our identity, the consolidation of our structure, for by maturing we are prepared for all wars, knowing how to bear the afflictions and contain the euphoria in victories, without ever changing our lives for change."

The Legacy

The dew falls from the sky, the sun shines and a new day comes,
The tears have already trickled down into the bowels of my being,
I change the dictionary from an ordeal and use the strength I have to overcome,
Every day there is a new decision to be made, but nothing can extinguish the flame that burns
To remember that I live to win and not be defeated,
Because the power begins when you reject being shot down.

Nothing guarantees victory; you will hear more than one,
But in me you are sure that I will win,
Losing the support of all and of the heart itself,
I use confidence to invigorate the treasure I have received,
Nothing conquers me, because I know that victory depends only on me.

In life pass people, places and things, only remains worthwhile,
Flee what is fleeting; perhaps your gaze saw the surrounding silence, the silence of solitude,
The absence that forced you to grow up not to depend on an illusion,
I erred and spoke what I should not have spoken, but I matured and realized that I can be forgiven. Changing with the force of repentance, remorse made me a slave to sin,
I was trapped for the pleasure of enjoying what I wanted every moment.
As much as they reject what I do, they cannot prevent me from moving forward,
Because I am guided by the certainty that I am strong enough to express myself
What I live, my work mirrors in my originality in assuming the truth
And to defend it in a real story, I have already identified myself with stories,
But my memories have a special flavour.

In life we fall, walk, err and sometimes hit,
But as human beings we make plans that take place if we are ready
To take our conviction to the last breath, until the last second,
Whoever dies, lives forever, because his legacy leaves his will to win,
For what was done and not for what remained to be done.

"We live in constant change and confidence makes us have the strength to overcome obstacles and to animate our soul against everything and against all, raising us from the ground and facing the world with the sword in hand without never giving up the victory."

Die and Live

I do not know how I'm still here today,
I shed many tears and blood of my soul,
With pains that have spread all over the conscience, I have not stayed a healthy part,
I am a corpse before a world that I do not belong to and I do not have the sense of my existence.

Many questions have arisen
And the answers he sought answered disappeared, but,
The more it submerged itself in the depths of discouragement,
I wanted to have more help, but I did not have it,
For no one can be helped without first helping himself.

In the dungeons I was frightened, in the ashes I was erased,
In the pains I have been inconsolable, in the losses I remained in mourning,
In the rest I remained the same on the outside, but weak in my interior,
Awaiting the consolation of God, a hug, affection, and a little love.

If in life I learned to stand alone,
It does not make sense to have friendships or clubs of appearance,
Because when we are on the ground and without feeling the beating of the heart,
Everything that was deemed ours shatters like a falling glass.
Without interference from any hand, if we are the problem in us
There may also be a solution.

There is no cure for pride, but the proud only disappear.
When you take your arguments out of hand and ask your permission to learn to be humble
And to practice repentance, for it is no use changing eternity
For a life of torment.

"Humility teaches to serve and arrogance to command, but what he serves gives what is best for himself and for others, but the arrogant loses his life by taking from others what he believes to be his, pride."

Incomprehension

Imagine this being the day you weep for the person you once were,
But that, with time gone, you cry for a dream in which you believe,
But on the inside, he died; you buried your soul in the dense depression,
You cry for help, but you only find misunderstanding.

In the density of darkness I encountered numerous questions,
I made a point of taking the time to meditate on the suffering and much advanced,
I cannot convince everyone to love me, but I can make my work known
And arouse the interest of crowds, I seek my recognition,
Made by effort, work and talent, for only victory has resurrected my being.
Fracassa who fights, cries who loses and wins,
Even if I lose and not be recognized,
I will not let myself be overwhelmed by discouragement,
I know that I have to live from a furnace in a furnace, treading stones and bearing bricks,

Using the pickaxe to dig my insides in order to pierce my pride,
Until I find humility in my heart, through the fire,
I will be able to deal with any situation,
Being subjected to any pressure.

In life it's good to know how to win and lose,
It is good to live in righteousness and to remain in truth, Even if it harms me for some time,
But have peace of mind and have peace to pursue,
Because today those who laugh at me will be those who in the crowds,
They will applaud and know that I have accepted to lose,
But to win is to fight without letting it succumb.

The pains, enemies, struggles and troubles come,
But I will remain strong to know how to resist the appeals of defeat,
The only answer I learned to give is the attack, I have no wedges,
I have no wealth, but I am sure that the dream that is in me will come true,
Because I will only give up when God is not able to hold my hand.

"No one has to understand or motivate us for the fulfilment of our dreams. The one who is sure to react, obey, sacrifice and persevere is us, and we only need silence to act in secret and to assume ourselves as responsible for our success or failure."

The Inner Change

A new year is celebrated, but nothing changes because you are in a new country,
Continent, city or house, I am strong to blame myself for my mistakes,
Love was a greatness that surpassed my fears,
Fighting was the only option to strengthen my weaknesses.

If I made a mistake today, I will not be able to amend it tomorrow,
The past does not come back, but I can change and build a new life,
If regret killed, then he would be dead,
Because I've cried countless times to erase the evil I've done,
But I have to go ahead and be with myself in peace.

The inexperience has accompanied me all my life,
But I do not blame her for all the evil I've done,
I know I'm wrong and do not ask for redemption, I'm willing to change and prove
That it is not only in speaking that one obtains forgiveness,
To act proves that it is better to be silent and let the attitude express my intention.

The years go by, but I still do not believe in the dream
I fed in my youth, the words uttered with attitudes
That they prove their purpose, they bring strength to weakness,
Bringing into existence what never existed, strengthening convictions,
Supporting hearts, giving life to those who no longer believe in happiness.

In little and not much,
Or even only when you have freedom to live in the dream world
That it is idealized in each consciousness, it is possible to be strong and overcome,
For death cuts off life, but does not invalidate faith, love, hope, and justice,
Even though I am mortal, I assume that I am happy.
And that I will fight for the happiness of those who suffer.

Even if life presents me with difficulties, they will make me grow,
If in this life I only have to content myself with smiles,
I will know that joy is not born when there is reason to smile,
But when I'm sad and I believe that everything will be fine,
Because I believe in what I do and I do not give space to what I see
It happens at certain times.

Even alone, I am the only one who can conquer the want; I have power to make my own decisions,
Choosing the outcome for my life, the pleasures, friends and riches,
If you have them, they will be scattered everywhere,
But I was born and will not have to do what I did, dream what I dreamed,
That it is what I am; I am special because in the universe I am an ideal being,
There is no one like me.

"The inner change gives rise to a new life, new results. It is not the places, things, and people that change our being; it is us, through sincere and true repentance."

The Seal of Love

You sealed within me and today only love burns when I think of loving once more,
It is a dance that surrounds me and whirls towards desired moments,
Demands that make my being more expensive, and in saying, I desire you without seeing you,
It's a pain I have, to love you without having you, to touch you without feeling your breath,
To lose myself in moments, but to always have your gaze to abandon reason.

I would call myself weak if I fought for an impossible love,
But I still have one chance, as much as I get tired,
However much the evidence is contradictory and the possibilities are scarce,
I will fight and I will leave to fulfil my end, I do not complain of the results,
But I will give back to the situation because I do not always agree to lose with the truth,
Even if she refers to no.

It is possible to love you without being with you,
It is possible to smell you without having you around,
It's possible to imagine myself on top of problems if I'm on the ground.
And to imagine that a word, gesture or a simple smile will help me
To obtain a solution through understanding,
Even though they do not understand me and realize what ails me.

I cannot abandon my responsibilities,
Although I leave my priorities to take care of myself,
I cannot live according to the world and what exists,
If I die, I'll have nothing to worry about on earth,
I live for myself and I die for what is secondary, my well-being is a priority.

Bombeias love to my soul and give me to drink with your attention,
For on the planet there is only one heart for a decision,
Loving you makes me sum up the universe in giving and loving without wanting to receive,
Fighting is my instinct, in front of what I think and what I feel.

I feel I have to react to survive, putting security at risk.
And make the change the most important part to be happy,
For rain does not fall in the same places, and the seas feed thousands,
So I nourish love, for in reason lies its root.

Before God, the world is dust that rises,
In front of me, difficulties are stairs that will elevate me to success.
And every second is evident the greatness of loving,
That is to do beyond what is requested,
Being present in more than what was requested,
Forgive even though being hurt; continue even wanting to give up,
Live when you want to die, fight and overcome limits, making defeat and victory
Elements that are the sustenance of those who want to win.

"The seal of love makes me walk on the water and not sink, go through the fire without burning myself, go through suffering and grow, use lost time as an instrument to become better and pain to sustain love with confidence and, in hopelessness, to believe in the impossible."

The Spirit of a Winner

When I think of giving up and letting myself be guided by illicit thoughts,
I become vulnerable in the face of situations, I think of the discouragement too
My emotions and let me float, drifting the worst,
I do not believe in anything else, and the life I have always considered sacred,
It becomes the heaviest stone to be loaded.

There are no people to comfort me, even injured, I have to continue,
Arranging solutions that persist in not appearing,
Being the solution and learning that reason makes me release the power,
That certainty is the trust that only I depend on to win.

It's hard to start over, but I have to get up,
I look for examples to be able to mirror myself,
But it's hard to find anyone who has not been corrupted
And pretending to live a life of appearances, Camoos died,
But today I am the living being in this generation at my disposal

It is fighting and overcoming what has happened, there is work, talent and dedication,
Against everything and against all of us, I walk with determination.

I am a prince of birth, of humble origin came my talent
And the suffering aroused the revolt that was in me, I was not born to shine,
But I have come to transform the concept that what is old is forever restored,
I am new but I do not feel intimidated to occupy
My place in the hierarchy of the victors.

I admire who conquers, but changing my identity makes me the bush that burns
And that does not consume you, because I love the truth and for me,
It is an insanity to corrupt me to live years of success
And an eternity of suffering, because to be a winner it is not enough to have talent,
I am forged in suffering and try even when I have not the heart to be the best,
Because having my personality requires not being content to be humble
With regard to poverty of spirit.
A real man creates himself in the battles, and I am ready to fight,
Sure, my success lies in what I believe will happen.

And not what I'm just seeing, because for me there is only one verb: to win!

"Winning is my priority and not an option. I only get the results that exceed my satisfaction, because when I am satisfied, I am conformed, I stop being conquered, I am discontented and I want more and more."

A Word to Say

Life fills me with the hunger to live, with the thirst of wanting to win,
To love and to give without waiting to receive, for I know that loving requires
All my devotion with so much joy pounding my heart,
With love, I assume my mission to love and to fight to be happy,
No word can describe what I intend to do,
But with my mind I am able to create and with my hands, execute a dream,
Exposing a talent, representing love has been a breath of fresh air.

As an angel I called the stars to give light, illuminating the sky,
I flew quickly to find the flame that burns me with desire to live,
Evil cannot prevail, for with our attitude we can change
The world without a word pronounce, examples are the perfect form
To turn love into justice, that seduces and makes us stop.

To think about what has been done, therefore, even all being flawed,
Love makes us see each one as a perfect being.
There is no hope without trust, there is no future without a present,
But there is forgiveness and repentance which
What has been destroyed in a lifetime, life assumes that each one is responsible
For what it does, and so it is the result of the decisions we have made,
For we live with success or failure.

As an angel, I know that I have no limits, as mortal, I know that I am subject to restrictions,
But my convictions allow me to drill depths,
Break limits and overcome the impossible because I see myself as I want to be
And I do not put the problem as an obstacle, but as an indicator of the shortest distance
Between wanting and doing, because I am a fighter and out of love, I will never stop fighting to win.

The years grow old because I am in the condition of a human being,
But on the inside I'm stronger, I challenge my talent and I do not fear death,
I learned to be strong in difficulties, when there was no reason to fight,
When nothing was foreseen, but I use poetry as an instrument,
I print love in inspiration, because I still have a word to say.

"Those who live by their dreams become the dream of someone who has, at the very least, the same level of demand to charge for themselves, for if we have the inspiration and the work, it is enough to trust to overcome the impossible, because our biggest challenge is not to start but to continue to go further and do more than what is required."

The Forgiveness

I said what I did not want to say, I got angry, losing my mind,
But I am heartbroken, I am hurt, but I want redemption,
I am submissive to reason, I do not control the emotion and I cry, I lose control of my being,
Tears are the expression I find to convey what I have to say.

I am a mere mortal, but what I did was optional,
I am not an ideal being for pretences, I am sensitive to pain and suffering,
I give time to the burial of the pain, I react, letting love clean the wounds,
Expel sorrows and rinse the tears of disappointment.

We cannot go back in time and erase the moment of ingloriousness,
They are words that do not go back, gestures that hurt more than physical aggressions
And that they corrode the soul, I beg to be calm, that calms me and makes me realize,
That everyone misses and nobody can be perfect.

To yield is to know how to forgive the guilty and, even if hurt, to accept reconciliation,
Nothing will be forgotten, but to have a clean heart is to make the enemy a friend.
I gain by example and not by word, for much is said, but little has been done,
Forgiving is the medicine I prescribe.

Forgiveness requires change, but there is always hope
Of peace, of mind and conscience which is priceless,
And nobody is worthy if they do not know how to give
First donate, without expecting something in return,
For we are what we do and our attitudes are the memorial that dictates our history,
For he who humbles himself obtains, in truth, humility and glory.

"Forgiveness quickens the spirit and the soul, benefiting all, sorrow only kills who carries it in itself, who carries it is who is accustomed to receive and not to give without waiting to receive."

The Impossible Dream

My soul charges me for its fulfilment,
I live to reach perfection, but in my heart,
I think I can give more, go further,
Living to win, but I need to fight without losing my head.

The ones do not make me stay strong,
To make my inspiration more awake,
To do more than is requested,
Do not be early to fear and it is no secret
That the dream is love, is life, my meaning!

I can run away all my life or have a little of everything, Being
a writer is my fate, and if it is not,
I end up becoming crazy.

I breathe poetry night and day,
I work to live forever
In the body and mind of those who want to know
That love is fire that produces heat
In the book of who lives what he intends to say.
In words I describe success,
But I deserve nothing, I do for being able

From assuming that I like war,
For I know only how to fight and desire to win.
I want to breathe and enjoy the work I do,
But when none of this happens, I'd be happy to think
That I conquer my space, because I struggle to be different,
Imagine if everything were the same, you would be the first to flee
And quitting would be the ideal option.

Today or I die fighting for my dream.
Or I die for accepting the accommodation,
In my conscience it is better to accept the truth
And face each difficulty, surpassing the no.

The dream makes me go after the invisible,
Materializing the certainty that my walk is not in vain,
For the impossible happens when it comes into being,
I will not fail to fulfil any of my words.

"The dream requires total surrender to the person who wishes to achieve it, making it the only and sufficient solution to all their problems, without needing third parties. He who is afraid also knows how to overcome him."

Love Tears

There are many tears that I shed for you,
I value love and, in the midst of pain, there is no end
For your defaults, because of you
I lost hours, months, years and lived torments.

At first impression you seem innocent in your way of being,
But time reveals that you do not show yourself to be what you're saying,
But I only suffered because I wanted to get involved with you without thinking
In the consequences that impel me to danger.

I'm strong, but I'm lost when you say you do not love anyone,
Men do not pay, but sometime later,
You make a life to two and I'm alone,
Because I believed in your intentions,
But your attitudes are summarized by various interpretations.

You do not deserve a tear or even my pain,
You sell at any price, you do not deserve
May I suffer for you for love.

Choices feature the person,
To love without thinking is to walk without looking,
At the risk of being a snack
From someone who just wants to use and throw away,
For a minute or an hour,
Who knows, if only for now.

Life requires you to move on,
Regardless of what was left behind,
I can be resistant, because failure does not satisfy me.

There is faith, confidence and perseverance to replace false friends,
For those who fight always reach the change that ends
In the habit of trusting without restraint,
I put my life at risk when I know
That I do not read with mere speculations.

"The intelligence associated with love makes a person valued and does not waste time with distractions that endanger his life, because it knows to guide us to the whole truth and gives us the strength to say yes to the indispensable and not to which is despicable."

Flames and Certainties

We are flames that go on in uncertainty,
To burn any impurity and clear the certainty
That moves us to make a decision,
Be a seal of love that stands firm
Against pain, suffering and disappointment.

We know how to bear the pains of injustice,
We live by what we want and not by what we feel,
Our feelings are pure and genuine,
My love is from a man who has loved you since childhood.

I wanted to have control of the sky and manifest myself with greatness and power,
To find my place without ceasing to realize that in order to have you,
I will have to fight and face all kinds of betrayals,
That come from where I did not feed my superstitions.

For you I built my world on the basis of the requirement of perfection,
With every beat of my heart my emotion increased,
But, using reason, I considered myself imperfect and worthy to evolve,
For you are able to love my faults, to boast of your deeds,
And one of them is to love, using weaknesses, so that, through them,
Grow up and stop thinking about quitting.

I know what I know because I needed to learn to listen first,
Having patience to understand, to offer and not to expect to receive,
This is the secret that makes me overcome the fear of conquering
Without having anything to lose.

Life teaches me to cherish the simplest things,
The little that I considered possessing is very much for me today,
I learned to value life, to make decisions,
And one of them is to offer my power to be able to
Capture and take you to like my inspirations.

"Life is the greatest gift you have. The greatest power that exists is the decision and, based on it, life assumes its form and identity, being faithful to the success or failure that are seen within the one who professes them."

Fight for Love

I get lost in a dream that haunts me to sleep and when I'm awake,
I love to leave my mark and live always to surpass my desires,
Living beyond the dreams I dreamed, living to fight and have more
Than what I've ever wanted.

Tears contain sadness, attitudes bring overcoming,
A practical man is stronger than an army.
And then a man of prayer,
Through weaknesses we improve, with the virtues we are accommodated,
With troubles we awakened forces that were asleep.

I want the time to stop and the rain to stop,
Fighting and overcoming my fears,
Underscoring my secrets,
Struggling to fight and go beyond
Of my limits, of my weaknesses,
For I am the one who thinks and the power is immense
To choose to fight and win, to love and to give.

In life I fight against everything and against all,
But with my dream I will expand my vision,
Because nothing prevents me from conquering when I imagine
That everything is possible when I use my determination.

I can be rich or poor, I do not care for mortals,
I was born to win, I fight for instinct and not for power,
What I have to say is express what I'm going to do,
For my profession is to be a fighter,
For I do not live without love.

"Fighting express initiative, movement, those who struggle move their life towards success, at risk of winning or losing, having the power to turn the no into the yes. Those who struggle have nothing to be ashamed of, prefer to die than to live with shame or accommodation."

The Use of Reason

Time goes by and there are no memories left,
Steps are stepped up and hopes are raised
Of seeing a light to illuminate such dense darkness,
But I live to fight, I'm wrought for wars.

Tears do not make you less than anyone,
They run down and shed all the load unloaded into a fatality,
Only then you see who is who, but it's good to always know the truth,
Sincerity is a balm to my wounds.

Sincerity is seen as a virtue or curse,
I use my head without going mad, listening to the heart,
I do not regret what happened, but I go on,
For I am determined to go on, to insist and to live.

I prefer to love and sacrifice my heart,
Do not give in to the emotion, I know it only remains
Who decides to use life for the benefit of intelligence?
For to be absorbed by temptations causes it to fall
At the height of stupidity and die one day at a time.

When change of conduct increases the dispute for me,
But if I am stubborn about my end,
If you insist on fighting and not escaping the pressure,
I prove that one has life in what is, some who use the faith
To explain what sometimes has no explanation.

"To use reason requires continuous exercise to be a servant of intelligence and not master of oneself. He who has dominion over himself is able to deal with great responsibilities, because he is able to organize his life in the first place."

The Life of Peace

In life I laugh against the current, I am a poet and I know that I am different,
Each morning is an opportunity to see the light of life,
Feel the wind blowing in my face, feeling the lightness of peace,
Nothing in life pays for a quiet and fulfilled life.

When I was a child, I valued wealth,
He loved to be noble and to have fame, profit and royalty, Life can end in a second, the aspirations
They are brief emotions that deceive and make the world The best friend, but it's inside the heart.
That lies the real danger.

Today, I know that life boils down to what I am,
What I think and what I do, but I always wanted to have time,
To decide what to do, to put things in proper place,
But wisdom does not make you wise, you become wise when
You use wisdom at all times, even if it contradicts
Your wills and give up your feelings.

People wanted to know everything, but they cannot predict death,
They wanted to have control of the world, but only the strongest,
Pass the idea that happiness is to have beauty, wealth and prestige,
But they cannot buy love and read their last day in the letters,
Because of illusions people are tired, I present you the poetry.
In life there is the right and the uncertain,
But nothing is the same if we persist in change,
For it demands from each one the price of victory,
From me I receive results, but to God I give honour and glory.

Humility is the essence of wisdom,
Pride is the principle of destruction,
Even if truth-telling puts an end to life,
There is always a way out when we know how to be firm
And posture to know how to say yes and no,

In afflictions we reap the respect,
In humiliations the pride is broken,
In the hard lessons we learn to obey,
For our lives do not mirror what the lips speak,
But the attitudes that reveal what we intend to do.

"We cannot deceive our conscience, but if we make it our friend, we have peace with us and we have the paradise inside us, even if, outside, we face wars."

Mistrust

I know it's hard to believe in you when there's only mistrust,
You live in a world that believes more in misfortunes, and, for
That you work, people insist on stifling your hopes,
But only you have the final word that decides the direction of your life.

In the family there is not always support,
Friends sometimes just give you a jerk up the middle of the road,
But it is we who must have the strength to carry on,
When others fall, I get up, because I do not have to give up.

There is in me a force that consumes me and gives me breath,
In poetry together work with the talent to dedicate myself
All the time and every moment makes me cry out the heart.

I have to get to where I can, do what nobody else does,
For in life only does not fight who is dead or settled,
You will not be happy for being dedicated or for being in love,
In life the price is paid, when you assume this fight you see what you want to see,

Fight bravely and release your power, which enables and empowers you,
To give you the conditions to overcome yourself and the most qualified.

I may fall, but I will never run away, I can be betrayed,
But I will not give up fighting, because the war cries out for me,
I am not a man of passivity, but to conquer my happiness
I use truth and mourning to overcome myself, for I know what I am capable of.

In life I only counted on the support of my parents,
My life is guided by perseverance, I fight against hope,
Because everything has an expiration date, but love makes me strong
To overcome my fears and defects, conquering immortality.

"When there are suspicions our strength must be greater to overcome everything, all and our weaknesses, because only will be standing that prove that his dream is a living reality and not an illusion, which comes down to the imagination that is not put into practice."

The Life of a Champion

I use my life to sacrifice myself for my dream,
I shed sweat, dedication and tears of a champion,
Who resisted and insisted to counter more than a no,
Ignoring my heart, I did not listen to the emotion.

I put my faith in my hands and I
Overcoming all that stubbornness in resisting,
Insisting is the materialization of my prayer.

I walk the path, even if I have to stop myself,
The words I could use to describe my story
They would show my faults and defects, because a champion
Do not use falsehood to hide your personality.

I wanted to hear voices of support, comfort,
But I only had my hope to recover my breath,
Resisting discouragement and depression,
I reassured my heart, proving that my strength
It is not in my quitting, but the persistence
It's the science that explains that I'm a winner.
Who uses love to communicate with mind and heart.

It is the rejections that strengthen me to continue,
It is the temptations that put my ambitions,
For I draw strength from weakness, for he who has all things but is lost in the world,
He is weak and needs help because he lives in illusion, if he dies he will lose his dignity,
For those who remember him will regret his last state,
And, in the last case, they will be lost, because they follow the voice of the heart.

But as a champion, I do not give up my rights,
I accept my faults, I correct myself more than necessary, I have much to learn, but if I weaken,
I will not fail to learn, for my dream lifts me up,
Even when I no longer have the strength to fight.

"The champion does not only overcome his personal struggles, but he conquers himself, because the real struggle is fought on the inside, which shows that life is the result of what has prevailed, or certainty or doubt."

The Power of True Dream

The stars showed me the myriad desires I have,
The dreams that I intend to realize, for strength is born in what I imagine,
In what I wish to possess, for I do not seek out what makes me happy,
But I believe I have the power to create what may exist.

The dream beats stronger than the heart,
For arise, even if you are fallen,
Strengthen yourself when you are weak,
Encourage yourself when you are discouraged,
Give yourself strength to overcome whatever,
Be sick of the spirit, of the soul,
Or even a disappointment of love.

You can face crowds for a dream,
But it is your dream that makes you different from others,
Who call the brave fools, believing in the impossible,
But who do what is not asked of them to realize dreams, to awaken the power that lay dormant in itself.

In the conquest of a dream wins who gives more of himself in everything,
Turning your back on the world and making every second an opportunity
To accomplish everything you want to conquer, because in life only prevails
Who is tired of suffering, who is tired of fighting is dead
Without realizing it, but does little of the one who was born to win.

"Dreams only live in those who are willing to everything for what they want to accomplish, because whoever believes in their potential is able to open the sky, to walk on the sea, to be able to have the sun in the palm of your hand and use the space as a ladder to explore your imagination, because the certainty that is in your heart makes him a champion."

The Greatness of Love

I love having the world in the palm of my hand,
I introduce myself as an admirer of love,
Due to its intense heat, I melt
Pure pleasure, sweetness and seduction.

I did not find explanations in the universe to express
In a nutshell, if loving can
May I be moved by my mother's courage,
Who created me, with what little he had,
He made me what I am today.

I do not want the world, because I only desire the faithful, But
I want each poem to fill the four corners with light
And that it be directed to the four winds to express greatness,
Knowing to forgive and give without waiting is the true meaning
From the beauty of love, which does not boil down to emotions or feelings,
He is intelligent because he uses his mind to speak his thoughts.

There is no greater force that causes God to manifest Himself,
For justice, truth and love go hand in hand
Alongside people embracing good moral principles,
That flesh and blood and corruption shall not inherit,
But he that is righteous shine like the sun in his might.

Of kisses and hugs I filled who loved,
With attitudes it proved that true was every word that said,
But in the poetry I express myself with delicacy and, with the pen in hand,
I am certain that love does not choose people, language or nation.

"Love involves the silence of an attitude taken in favour of those who do it liberally without expecting anything, because love drives us to not be satisfied with what we give, we strive to give more and more and always do our best in our and in favour of others."

The Truth of a Dream

When I hear the waves crashing against the rocks,
I see the intensity that every poem, every dream makes to come to the world,
When I float on the waters, I see myself before the greatness of God.

The simplest things in life denote the seal of perfection,
But when a mighty man rises up for battle,
It has the power to subdue the sky, the earth, the universe and the sea,
For his action shows revolt and decision.

In life everything happens to exist when you imagine,
And the dream is a living reality that moves the brain,
It forces me to make decisions, I think of each reader,
For I, with all the affection and love, prepare each verse,
To express the greatness of my convictions.

I am a human being, but I see myself as a conqueror,
I do my job with all the dedication,
Every dream is a heart that pumps life,
The impossible is what I dream to achieve, for I know that I can
Go beyond my limits and increase my strength.
Love is translated into several languages,
But only he understands who accepts him intelligently,
I am a man who follows what he thinks and does not live
For what he feels, because to suffer for love is the appetizer of the heart,
He is the translator of a life of sadness, pain and disappointment.

When I do not live by what I see and by what I feel I have peace,
For every bad news is a bomb that explodes for the one who hears
Without sorting out what he sees, hears, thinks and speaks.

I believe in me,
Even if they do not think me capable of being great,
I can be the best poet because I do not conform
In being one more than here passed, I know of my value,
I fight for myself, for life and for love, and nothing extinguishes the pain
From a heart full of revolt, which wants to fight and win,
In order to be a generator of life and greatness.

To lose is to accept everything or do the same things,
To act is the force that impels me to guarantee what I desire
And even with my requests taken, I'm not satisfied,
Because I know that many need me, and I need to be strong,
For my story will last forever, I do not depend on luck.

"Incentives come from our dreams. The way we see ourselves determines who we are and what our life will be, because whoever looks great, lives, sleeps, wakes, struggles and insists until he reaches where he wants and wants to go beyond his limits."

The Usefulness of Life

I pass by everywhere and I see that it is good to live,
I want to win, to walk among the stars,
Fly and spread the dream that haunts me,
The fire that burns me constantly,
I sleep, I wake up and I fight to be what imagines my mind.

I cannot change my past,
I can react and decide to be different,
The glory is to change who I am,
Vã is the hope of living splendidly
With riches or with pride, everything ends one day,
Because all the craziness ends when our stay ends.

There is no time to always ask forgiveness,
But there is time to think about every decision,
In every dream and every word, so life is spent,
Fuelled by the incessant search of filling
That the heart feeds on the illusion of not wanting to hear no.

It is time to think that there is no end,
For us is reserved what we gave by the most important, Will it be the goods, the fame, the family or our own self?
What will make us fall into the illusion that one day our life is lost?
As much as it receives applause or the silence of who ignores me,
I make time to repent and change my history,
Giving all of me what I do and what I believe,
Because I live with poetry wanting to leave, wanting to transmit
That living is doing more than just fulfilling our requests.

"We are happy in what we give and not in what we just receive. Time can be an ally or enemy of ours, each of us is responsible for its outcome, even if it has not chosen to come to this world, because the power of decision is the greatest gift that each one has."

Love

I do not have roses to give you,
I have no diamonds that can spark your greatness,
But with my lips, I can say that there is no one
Compare yourself with my hands, I can write and describe
The love I feel, the admiration of loving you, more than life,
No vein can get through the fire of sacrifice,
Passion is illusion and emotion makes the heart a waste.

With all due respect, nothing is worth it if you do not exist, I live to have you in my arms, nothing has value
If I do not have you, if I do not kiss you, I'll lose my will. Of making any wish, but the truth I have to assume,
For you I am capable of loving and ignoring the verb to give up.

You are the sky to me, I go up to see
Your immensity, you make me have the sensation of travelling in time,
Eternity is a happiness because there is no hurry and anxiety
And the truth makes every second and minute a moment
Of tenderness, of love, of fervour, spreading to the four winds

That I am made of flesh and use intelligence, but I have feelings.
I need more of you than the air to breathe,
Loving is more important than drinking water,
For I depend on inspiration, which gives the heart Evidence that anything is possible,
When you really love, when you give your life,
Love is reborn and everything blossoms naturally.

"Love brings life and is the force capable of transforming us completely, because love is based on attitudes and not on words. A life with luxury and without love is a body full of splendour, but it has no spirit that gives it life."

The Difficult Times

There are times when I feel like crying,
Drop everything and hide from the world,
The pain persists in not disappearing,
Alternatives are studied if
Going beyond it all ends.

Words and actions are not erased,
But we can move forward in time,
Determined not to make the same mistakes,
Overcoming the fears, because there has to be a confrontation,
For a life is about to be decided.

I have strength to overcome my limitations,
I understand that I cannot be good at all,
But I take every second to improve,
After all, learning is a gift that makes me wise.

There are times when everything seems to make no sense, I
follow my convictions to contradict the suggestions
That emotions blow in the mind and in the ear,
Only my decision can put an end to the situation.

Out of love, I do not judge and do not do justice with my own hands,
But it hurts to be wronged and to live as if it were iron,
But it is on the basis of the difficulty that a real man is born.

You cannot wait against time,
For men and women want their emancipation
Without using humility as a collaboration of learning
That is achieved throughout life, not a brief moment.

When I do what has not been done, I discover the strength I possessed,
Although not perfect, each defect becomes an indicator
Of continuous improvement, which turns weakness into strength and power,
Each one has in his hands the best option to decide what he wants to be.

"Only the worst difficulties are overcome when one decides to confront and act against what one feels and thinks, because our conscience evaluates and decides based on intelligence and it is in it that our battlefield resides because, in order to move definitively, the greatest step is the change of thoughts."

The Power of Imagination

It is the struggles that motivate me to awaken my imagination,
Using it to idealize my desires, being small, I can be great,
If you decide to let the dream that is within me go out, I am strong, insistent,
I do not settle for what they think and say against my ideals,
For my thoughts reveal that my feelings are
Inscribed in the poems and in the heart of those who want to love more and more.

I begin to think of standing before God and, glimpsing the Universe,
Before his throne, I write the wonders of creation in verse,
For love is a balm that heals the wounds of the soul, when I am alone,
I like to walk and see the sea, which can express tranquillity,
It is a source where the perpetual beginning of the greatness of my ambition arises,
For I give myself to the poetry of body, soul and heart.

It's not words or bad people
That they will destroy my dreams, for I live in secret,
I cancel the fear and I leave in silence, conscious that the victory is in me,
Imagination makes me see my dreams and gives me the certainty that they will come true
In models of courage and life for those who wish to take inspiration from someone.

There are no barriers, currents, storms and lightning strikes
Who decides to fight and conquer what he desires and, even if he has to insist,
It does not give up the desire that longs to give birth and spread greatness,
For the beauty of someone is in their inner strength.

The winner did not choose where he was born,
He did not choose his parents or his social status,
But his revolt gives rise to a certainty that defies all its limits
And face everything, putting your life at risk, because suffering is optional.

If all the poor men told their vision,
Everyone would give money, because today they are rich,
Because they gave up everything in favour of their imagination,
They fought without seeing anything, but believed in their potential,
I believe that even when I write, I will be a great poet,
For I transmit what I desire, and what I long for is your satisfaction,
Make this poem an impulse for the dreams you have in your heart.

"The imagination allied to the disposition and the intelligence makes any person strong, capable around that which distresses him, firm in front of everything and everyone, for his strength is based on his convictions, and his thoughts bring to existence the non-existent, because she wished, fought and insisted that this "son," her dream, come to the world because she decided that each one makes her story and not that circumstances make each other's life what it has been."

The Fellow Love

I slept, but I dreamed of you,
My breath tried to breathe in a new breath,
But every moment that I passed with you invaded my thought,
I tried to resist,
But the more I try to escape,
I'm stuck with your memory.

On my lips I feel the urge to tell you
In my life there is only one word to say,
Love is what I feel for you, I try to resist,
But he lives as a part of me.

I waited against the longing,
But the truth is that I remain attached to you,
In dreams, in memories,
Waiting against hope,
Suspicious of mistrust,
I breathe against longing.

In death we are immortal,
In sorrow we cry,
Because we want to love more,
We know that our union is true,
Because I love you as if I knew you all my life…

"True love presents us and fights side by side with those who live and prioritize it, making death, time and difficulties their greatest victims, for it is eternal, cannot be extinguished."

The Power of True Love

I can stop the time and caress your face,
Looking into your eyes more than once,
I find the truth in the depths of your eyes,
It is possible to see the glow of the light of our love.

Sometimes we are distant,
But our pains are not worrisome,
We are friends, companions and eternal lovers,
We cover our bodies with fidelity,
In looking, thinking, speaking and acting,
For we are a wall that withstands all the pressures
Of the illusions that want to destroy us.

In our kiss it burns the desire to want always more,
Our life is linked to the purity of intelligent love
And we do not yield to carnal desires, even though we are mortal,

We are subject to weaknesses and corruptibility,
But we would rather give up the kiss of lies.
And prove the truth of truth.
We are the standard of happiness,
We strengthen our relationship with integrity,
We make the impossible possible in our daily lives and we execute our plan,
For work complements talent, we do not give wings to distractions,
We want to live away from gossip and other opinions,
For we have planned for our love to live, even if our hearts stop.

"True love is a novelty because it renews itself every day and transforms those who feed on it, because those who fully embrace the love and dream they dream of remain indestructible against everything and against all because they practice the oath they did to themselves and keep themselves from the corruption that plagues this world."

The Certainty of the Realization of Dreams

I cried many weeks for you,
But nothing erases the memory that I keep in me,
A love that I embraced with all my strength,
Even when he felt like giving up.

The tears come out, the pains spread through the body, But
the memories do not fade, the words
Do not go back, we swear to stay together,
Even if the fights required the most of us.

With our looks we have seen our overcoming,
With our kisses we gave certainty to the heart
That the battles will all be won,
Even if our certainties are hurt,
We will never cease to believe in the power of our conviction.

Even if my heart stops beating
I will never stop believing in our overcoming,
I give you my full attention and all that is needed,
But I just want you to stay with me and fight with me,
For you are the paradise with which I have long dreamed.

"Even if we do not see the fulfilment of our dreams when we want, it does not mean that they will not come true, because we fight for what we believe and not for what we see, for the winner is the one who fights when he goes through the tribulations, not just on good occasions."

The Right Woman: God's Best Gift

I will not forget to love you again,
I lose myself with your smile, which melts me,
Your gaze marks a meeting with precision,
I am mesmerized by the language it conveys,
Even without giving a hint can say
That we love each other more than the love we had
As soon as we met for the first time.
I want to value you at every moment,

I do not want to get used to love,
I want our lives to be a new dawn every day,
For through you I can write to say that poetry
Renew my strength when I am weak,
I have love for my job and I fight taco
To win and stay on top of greatness.

You are the splendour of the universe,
I want to lose myself in this light that illuminates me,
You entice me when I am cold and insecure,
You take me out of the dark and dispel sorrow as if it were a mist,

You do not fight for lost, I always ask you lair,
You make me have love and respect for life.
I will not forget you in the cold of solitude,
In the midst of so many doubts you are the only solution
That dispels the fears and that makes me quiet,
I'm safe when I stop to listen
Your counsels, which are most precious
Than all the treasures of this world.

"The right woman is God's greatest treasure, because it is the right choice that makes life complete and full of accomplishments."

The Power of the True Dream

He liked the talent to be necessary for everything to be proven,
But I know that the work pays off any effort that is made,
For it shows my blood and dedication,
I am an angel, who came down from heaven with a mission,
Spread love as a message of overcoming,
For there is no use in making life a burden to bear,
Everything becomes easier when I do more than expected.

I had every reason to give up,
But I did not let myself down, even when I had no reason to smile,
I faced each battle as a finale in which I fight to win,
I know there are many writers, but I use my ambition
To prove that I am a specialist in heart will.

With humility I learned to challenge science,
I have discovered that a belief allows me to challenge the impossible
And for this reason, here I am, ready to show that I will not back down,
Because this poem is a bridge connecting the universe to the greatness of what I am,

A man who is dedicated to fighting for what he wants,
I'll fight to the end, whatever.
I will declare to the lost that there is salvation,
To my few friends you have only one option,
Follow me and move on, or, then, stay back,
From now on I am confident that I will show what I am capable of.

"Talent allows us to know the greatness of a dream that cries out for its fulfilment in the mind, the heart and, as a pregnant woman in pain, will do everything to be accomplished, because it is the force of the impossible that makes possible the desire of him who believes in himself and in his fulfilment, against everything and against all, by himself."

Made in the USA
Monee, IL
03 May 2026

49437787R00049